the final dance WORKBOOK

CHERYL DEINES, MSW

Editors:
Dale Metcalfe
Maureen Rafael

Cover & Interior Design:
Patricia D'Arrigo

Interior Design & Formatting:
Streetlight Graphics

The author of this book does not dispense medical advice nor prescribe use of any techniques as a form of treatment for physical, mental or emotional problems without the advice of a physician. The intention of this book is to offer information of a general nature to support you in your quest for emotional and spiritual well-being. In the event that you use any of the information in this book for yourself, the author and the publisher assume no responsibility for your actions.

ISBN-13: 978-1-7321400-1-1
ISBN-10: 1-7321400-1-4
Printed in the United States of America

Table of Contents

The Taboo Of Death

Orienting to Death

Dancing With Death

My Expansion

Final Thoughts

Healing Exercises

To the courageous souls willing to go on this personal exploration in order to bring the lessons from *The Final Dance* into your lives. As you apply these profound teachings may you expand and embrace life more fully.

Acknowledgements

To my friends, family, hospice patients and bereavement clients. Thank you for showing me what love really looks like.

Introduction

Allow this creative exploration to be your dance partner as you gently explore your current reality and where you can see opportunities for expansion. The additional questions and exercises in *The Final Dance Workbook* will give you the opportunity to shift your life experience or to see how brilliantly you have already created your life. Be kind to yourself through this process, acknowledging your successes as well as the areas where you are not yet where you would like to be. They are all opportunities to gain clarity and to move more fully into authentic self-expression. Each experience you have in life is an opportunity to allow more and more of your true essence to shine through.

The Taboo Of Death

Demystifying Death

Only when you accept that one day you'll die can you make the best out of life. And that's the big secret. That's the Miracle.

~Gabriel Ba~

In the first chapter of *The Final Dance* there is discussion about how death is perceived through the media and how this depiction utterly confuses the truth about death. We look at mainstream American views and how they avoid the topic of death. There is also discussion about the gifts and benefits available to those who are able to push past their fears and face the reality that they will someday die. We begin to gently explore our feelings and beliefs about death knowing that this exploration can enrich our lives if we chose to go on this journey of self-discovery, applying the lessons that only death can teach us in order to more fully embrace life. The ultimate goal is to get to the end this life without regrets. The reality is that we are all "terminal." Some of us just have a better idea of when death will occur. It takes courage to turn and face any fears or discomfort you may have. Use the journaling exercise and the questions on the next few pages to begin this exploration.

Journaling Exercise: I would encourage you to simply "sit" with your feelings about dying and write about what comes up for you. Are there questions, fears, feelings that come when you think about death? Write about them. This activity will support you on getting clear about what you believe, as well as identifying any questions you might have.

Allow the questions on the next few pages to take this exploration even deeper.

Questions to Dance With...

Do you ever allow yourself to think about dying? If so, what are your thoughts? If not, why do you avoid this topic?

What experiences have you had around death? Describe in detail.

How did these experiences impact your life?

What questions come up for you when you think about death?

Orienting to Death

Turning Toward Death

Sometimes what is in the way, is the way.

~Mark Nepo~

In this chapter I give an overview of my personal journey and the self-destructive path I was on prior to working with the dying. I include some of my spiritual history in order for you to see how my beliefs shifted through my experiences around death, including my lack of belief in life after death when I first began working in hospice. I share how my curiosity about different spiritual teachings increased and sent me on a personal quest for answers. May you find the answers you seek through your own exploration.

Questions to Dance With...

We all have our personal stories and challenges that impact our feeling and beliefs about life and death. What have been some of those experiences in your life?

How have those experiences changed the way you view or live your life?

Have you had a time in your life that you would consider a "turning point"? Describe it.

How did your life and beliefs change because of that experience?

Dancing With Death

Going Home

A butterfly lights beside us like a sunbeam and for a brief moment its glory and beauty belong to our world. But, then it flies on again, and though we wish it could have stayed, we feel so lucky to have seen it.

~ Author Unknown ~

Home Is Wherever You Are

During my time with Eleanor, I asked her if she was ready to go home. She responded, "Home is *wherever* you are." This statement resonated with me and has deepened as I have had more life (and death) experiences. So many of us are wishing our lives away, waiting for the weekends, a different job, to lose weight and on and on. We are powerful beings and when we focus on that which we don't want we are actually bringing more of the same into our lives. Relaxing into your current reality frees your energy to create and opens you to guidance. The questions on the next few pages can help you to explore this concept.

Questions to Dance With...

What does the statement "home is wherever you are" mean to you?

When do you feel most at home?

Write about any areas in your life that you are resisting.

What can you do to feel more at home in your current situation?

Seduction Of Safety

The greatest loss in life is not death.
The greatest loss is what dies inside us while we live.

~Norman Cousins~

Safety Is Overrated

In this chapter I share the story of Madeline and Klaus. They held a great deal of resentment, blaming each other for the outcome of their lives and wishing things were different in what appeared to be a loveless marriage. Their story was one of regret. Madeline felt trapped in a marriage she had chosen for safety. Klaus attempted to control Madeline. Yet he was unable to control what mattered most – how she felt about him. Both died unfulfilled and disappointed.

After my experience with Madeline and Klaus, I explored where in my life I was playing it safe. With this awareness, I was able to make different choices. May the next series of questions support you in a similar exploration.

Questions to Dance With...

Identify an area in your life where you feel discontent or feel like you have been settling. Write about it in detail.

What choices do you have regarding this situation? Write them down even if they are not ideal.

If you made these choices how might your life change? I invite you to use your imagination here.

What is one thing you can do today to begin to shift this situation?

Mothers and Daughters

Sometimes the strength of motherhood
is greater than natural laws.

~ Barbara Kingsolver~

Pay Attention To Your Dreams

This was one of my first experiences in which my bereavement clients shared that they felt their deceased loved ones had communicated with them. What really got to me that day was the fact that in a matter of a couple of hours I had been with two women who both firmly believed that their mothers had come to them at the moment of their death to say goodbye. Since then I have heard hundreds of stories like these, and became aware of the importance of paying attention to your dreams. As I began exploring my dream world, I would sit in silence in the mornings with pen and journal in hand, attempting to catch my dreams before they quickly flitted away. During that morning ritual, I received an unexpected gift. In those quiet moments before I fully engaged with life, I began to connect with more than just my dreams from the night before. I began to hear the whispers from my soul calling me forth into my life more fully.

Questions to Dance With...

Describe a vivid dream you have had. It could be about a loved one– or anyone or anything else that comes to mind. Describe it in detail. If you don't remember your dreams, write about a dream you have for your life.

What does this dream mean to you?

Describe a time when you felt that you received a message through your dreams.

What actions did you take as a result of this dream?

An exercise to play with...

Keep a dream journal. It is simple to do. Just keep a pen and pad on your bedside table. As soon as you wake up, sit in silence for a few moments to "be" with your dreams, writing down what you recall from the night before. The more you do this, the more easily you will remember your dreams. As you take this time each morning, you may find that it goes far beyond remembering your dream from the night before. That quiet time can also help you to connect more deeply with the longing of your soul.

Back to Life

We are all so much together, but we are all dying of loneliness.

~Albert Schweitzer~

We Need Each Other

In this chapter you met Florence, who appeared to be close to death. She had become isolated and lonely. Within a matter of days, as hospice staff and volunteers began making visits, she began to reengage in life. The daily visits motivated her to get up, get dressed and attend to her many "visitors." It was a powerful reminder of how we are impacted by the interactions in our lives and how important our connections with others can be. Allow the next series of questions to support you in exploring your own connections.

Questions to Dance With...

How do you feel about depending on others or asking for help?

Is there an area in your life where you could use support? Describe.

Who are the people in your life you can reach out to when you need support?

Describe a time when you supported another. Talk about how it made you feel.

If it made you feel good, remember this the next time you need support. Most people want to help.

Dressed for God

Attitude is a little thing that makes a big difference.

~Winston Churchill~

Our Attitude Impacts Our Experience

Greg demonstrated how powerfully his attitude impacted his life (and death). Greg's attitude remained positive in spite of his terminal diagnosis and the fact that he had to move to a nursing home. His ability to see the bright side in any situation resulted in his continuing to have pleasant experiences through the end his life. Just as a positive way of thinking and behaving can affect our lives, so can a negative approach. Sometimes we are so entrenched in our way of viewing life that we are not aware of how we are influencing our experience. Use the next series of questions to assess where you are without judgement. Awareness is the key. When we become aware of how our thinking impacts our life, we can begin to shift our way of thinking if it is not serving us.

Questions to Dance With...

Identify an area in your life that isn't working as well as you would like and elaborate on it. (finances, romance, creativity, etc.)

Write about some of the things you think or say about this situation.

Can you see any correlation between how you think or your attitude toward this situation and the outcome?

What gifts are in this experience? If my patients can find gifts in their dying process, I have complete faith that you can find the gifts that are imbedded in your challenges!

Winged Messages

If you aren't living in awe then you aren't paying attention.
~Dan Millman~

Be Vulnerable

In this chapter, I share a series of stories about the encounters that I and my bereavement clients have had with birds and butterflies after the death of a loved one, and how I have come to believe that those who have passed on can send messages to their loved ones from beyond the grave. I share how common these occurrences are, acknowledging the courage that it takes to share these experiences and how powerful it is to have these experiences validated by others having similar experiences. I invite those of you who have had synchronistic, mystical or unusual experiences to share them with others and to recognize what a vulnerable act this is.

Questions to Dance With...

Are there unusual experiences or coincidences you or someone you know has had around the death of a loved one? Write about it in detail.

What was your first thought or reaction after having or hearing about this experience?

What are your thought or feelings about sharing this experience with others?

Whom would you feel safe sharing with?

Guide Me Out of the Pain

Everybody needs beauty as well as bread, places to play in and pray in, where nature may heal and give strength to body and soul.

~John Muir~

Suffering Is Optional

In this Chapter I share my holy encounter with Lucy, who was immersed in her experience of pain. As I used guided visualization to shift her attention away from her pain, her experience of pain lessoned. It confirmed for me something I have heard many of my spiritual teachers say: What we focus on expands. For Lucy the focus was on her pain. I encourage my readers to notice what they are focused on any time they have the experience of suffering and then to shift their focus on to what they want to create, or what they are grateful for. The next series of questions will help you to explore this concept even further.

Questions to Dance With...

Is there something in your life that is causing you pain? It can be physical or emotional pain. Write about it in detail.

What are some of the thoughts you have about this situation?

List five things you are grateful for about this situation. Go ahead, I invite you to dig deep.

Bonus Exercise: Start a gratitude journal. It can be as simple as writing down five new things that you are grateful for every night before you go to bed. Try it for six weeks and watch for the inevitable shift in your level of joy.

Permission

If you love someone, you must be prepared to set them free.

~ Paulo Coelho ~

Freedom Occurs In Letting Go

I was reminded of the importance of freeing another as I supported Joanna and her father, Edward. For weeks Joanna had been begging her father to hold on, to stay. When she finally decided that holding on to him was not serving him, I again experienced how powerful freeing another could be. She gave him permission to go, and within thirty minutes he let go, after weeks of holding on. She realized that keeping him trapped in a body that was not serving him was not loving. I realized that by witnessing this encounter that sometime the most loving thing we can do for another is to set them free. I also shared a personal experience where I had released an intimate relationship in order to free us both. Are there places that you are holding when it is time to let go? Explore this further with the questions provided.

Questions to Dance With...

What or who are you holding onto that is no longer serving you? Describe this situation.

What is it that keeps you engaged with this person or situation? What are you getting or how are you benefiting?

What concerns do you have about releasing this situation or person?

What are you making space for by releasing this relationship or situation?

How might your life be different if you let go?

Ultimate Sacrifice

True love is selfless. It is prepared to sacrifice.

~Sadu Vaswani~

Let Love Decide

In Luella's story I was reminded of how strong a parent's love can be. From all appearances, it looked like Luella could have gone on for days longer. But she saw an opportunity for her children to be taken care of and chose to exit at that time. I have repeatedly been moved by the generosity, courage and sacrifice my patients make for their loved ones, often waiting until they know their loved ones will be taken care of before leaving their bodies. I have also seen my patients' families giving emotionally, energetically and financially in order to take care of their loved ones through the end of their lives. My faith in humanity has certainly been restored by witnessing these acts of love. We all have the ability to give in this way. And most of us probably have. Let the questions that follow clarify where love is expressed and received in your life.

Questions to Dance With...

What decisions or actions have you taken as a result of your love for another?

How did it feel to give so freely of yourself?

Describe an experience in which someone gave freely to you out of love?

Write about how it felt to have someone give to you so freely.

What holds you back from giving freely to those you love?

Existential Musings

Come, come, whoever you are, wonderer, worshipper, lover of leaving. It doesn't matter. Ours is not a caravan of despair. Come, even if you have broken your vow a thousand times. Come, yet again, come, come.

~ Rumi ~

Take Off The Armor

I felt so privileged to have had the experience I had with Frank as he gave his confession to me. His honesty and vulnerability at the end of his life moved me more than I can say. But I was also saddened to know he had spent many decades of his life protected by armor of his own making. It is not uncommon to build walls when we get hurt, and for a time those walls may be necessary, but when we continue to walk through life with armor on long after the trauma has passed, we are not able to connect with others. I encourage you to examine whether you have erected walls of protection. And if you have built walls are they still serving you? Be gentle with yourself through this process.

Questions to Dance With...

Write about one experience from your life that may have resulted in you wanting to protect yourself.

How did you respond to this experience? Did you build walls? Or make decisions about life or people? (You might not have been conscious of it until now).

How has this experience and the decisions you have made impacted your life and relationships?

If you have built walls to protect yourself, what steps could you take today to start removing the armor or tearing down the walls?

How do you feel about removing this protection?

Guru or Priest

Have patience with everything that remains unsolved in your heart. Live in the question.

~Rainer Maria Rilke~

Re-examine Past Beliefs

This was the story of Visha, a man who struggled at the end of his life. Raised Catholic, he had denounced his religion as a young man and embraced a different path for most of his life, following a guru from India. He was very devoted to his beliefs and his guru. Yet, at the end of his life, he appeared to hold on until he received the Catholic ritual of last rites. The teachings he learned as a child were imbedded in his psyche. Visha was seemingly unaware that he was still carrying those beliefs from long ago, but deep in his subconscious he held onto the beliefs and could not "let go" of this life until he had received last rites. It is common to develop beliefs at an early age and live from those decisions. Allow the next series of questions to assist you in exploring where in your life you are holding on to beliefs and decisions made at a young age. Only you can determine whether these beliefs continue to serve you.

Questions to Dance With...

Can you remember the first time in your life as a child when you felt that you were not safe? Or that you had been deeply hurt or traumatized? Describe this memory.

Describe any decisions about life, people or yourself you may have made at that moment? (You might not have been conscious of it until now).

How has your response or the decision you made impacted your life?

Does this belief serve you? Or is it time to let it go?

If you do feel you need to release this story, what is a "worthy" story or belief you can replace it with?

Create a list of positive statements or affirmations you could make to help to cement this new way of thinking about yourself (i.e. I am lovable, I am beautiful, I am powerful, etc.).

Now post the most powerful statement on your bathroom mirror (or the one that is hardest for you to believe).

Between Worlds

The most beautiful thing we can experience is the mysterious. It is the source of all true art and science.

~Albert Einstein~

We Are More Than Our Bodies

In this chapter, I share a series of stories that show examples of the different phenomena I have experienced in my work with the dying. These include expanded awareness, in which my patients appear to be aware of more than what they can humanly know, such as the conversations heard from across the house by Rose (who was stone deaf), or awareness of their loved one's death when no one has told them. I also share examples of deathbed visions in which those who are terminally ill see deceased loved ones and spiritual figures. And my experience with Sean, who seemed to transcend his mental illness at the end of his life. These experiences were reminders to me that we are so much more than our physical bodies. The next series of questions will give you an opportunity to explore your personal beliefs.

Questions to Dance With...

When people talk about having a soul, what does that mean to you?

Do you believe that there is a part of us that lives on after we die? Say more about this.

What is your sense of why people go through challenging situations in life?

Old Blue Eyes

Don't ask what the world needs. Ask what makes you come alive, and go do it. Because what the world needs is people who have come alive.

~ Howard Thurman ~

Never Stop Dancing

Unable to write or talk, Tom was not able to communicate with me in the normal way. I had to trust my instincts as I supported him in exploring his fears. I again experienced the power of being be fully present with another human being. Although Tom could only answer yes and no questions by squeezing my hand, so much more was communicated just by his eyes. He reminded me through our final dance together how much joy we can experience in simple acts. I encourage you to explore what it is that makes your heart sing.

Bonus Activity: Spend an evening with a loved one without words. Use your creativity to communicate with each other, staying fully present to ensure that you don't miss anything.

Questions to Dance With...

What brings you joy?

What stops you from having more pleasure in your life?

What steps can you take to bring more of that which "lights you up" into your life?

What is one thing you could do today that would bring you joy?

Sins of the Son

The heart of a mother is a deep abyss at the bottom of which you will always discover forgiveness.

~Honoré de Balzac~

Truth Is Within You

This was the story of Chandra, who struggled at the end of her life because her son Tyrrell had died by suicide. Her struggle was a direct result of what she had been told by the priest in the Catholic Church she attended. She was told that her son would not be in Heaven when she got there because he had committed an "unforgivable sin." As we explored her feelings and beliefs, she came to her own conclusion. She often felt God's presence and described him as a loving father who wanted the best for his children. Through this exploration she came to *know* that the loving, compassionate God that she had come to know and love would never abandon a child during his lowest point in life. When she came to this realization, she *knew* that she would see her son again. I believe that she connected to the internal guidance that is within us all. When we hear Truth, we know it at a cellular level. Chandra stopped taking someone else's word as truth and found the answers that she needed within her. Allow the next series of questions to help you to explore what you believe.

Questions to Dance With...

Do you believe in a God or a Higher Power? If so, write about the characteristics of this God. If not, say what you do believe in and write about that.

Are there mainstream spiritual beliefs or teachings that don't resonate with you? What are they, and where do you disagree with them?

Are there religious or spiritual teachings from childhood that you have been carrying that no longer serve you? Or other beliefs that no longer serve you?

As you have examined your beliefs about spiritual teachings, are there fears or feelings that have come up around "questioning your beliefs?" Explore those thoughts and feelings.

Write about the spiritual or religious teachings that you resonate with, the teachings that feel like Truth to you.

Golden Light

Faith is the strength by which a shattered world shall emerge into the light.

~ Helen Keller~

Give Others Your Undivided Attention

In the story *The Golden Light*, I share my experience with Karen. I was privileged to be with her in the last hours of her life and midwifed her through her death. I remained fully present with Karen and adjusted what I was doing with her based on her responses. From that place of presence, I was able to experience something I had never been aware of before when sitting with a patient as they died– her soul leaving her body. Often when I am with a patient, my energy and focus are split, as I am also supporting family. But because of Karen's circumstances and her husband's inability to be there with her, she had my undivided attention.

Questions to Dance With...

Describe a time in your life when you were fully present to another.

Are there areas in your life where you know you are "distracting" yourself rather than fully engaging? Pick one and describe it.

How might it be different if you were fully present?

What is one thing you can do right now to disconnect from distractions?

Identify one person you long to connect more deeply with:

What are some things you can do to be more present with this person?

Challenge: I challenge you to try non-distraction for a day— to be fully present with those you love. Unplug ... be available ... listen fully ... and be aware of how your interaction is impacting other people. Then watch the magic happen.

Dancing Queen

Silence becomes cowardice when occasion demands speaking out the whole truth and acting accordingly.

~Mahatma Gandhi~

Speak Your Truth

Crystal was an unlikely teacher for me. Initially, I saw her as rude, demanding, and entitled. But I came to appreciate her direct, honest communication. Although her honesty was not always delivered in the kindest way, I saw the benefit of this clear communication. I always knew where I stood with Crystal. And in the end when she felt the need to "clean things up" before she died, I witnessed a rawness and vulnerability that all too often is missing in human interactions. I watched her take responsibility for her actions and let people know where she felt wronged or misunderstood. These relationships deepened before my eyes.

Seeing how cleanly she communicated with people resulted in me pausing to look at my own communication style. Being a lifetime people pleaser, my communication style was much more passive, indirect and less honest. Use the following questions to explore your communication style.

Questions to Dance With...

Are there situations in your life where you are being less than authentic? Where are you saying "yes" when you want to say "no"? Describe how you communicate.

What are your concerns about setting boundaries and being totally honest with others?

Is there anyone you are blaming for something that is going on in your life? If so, who and why?

Describe where you might have played a part in creating this situation. (Remember, there is freedom in taking responsibility where you can.)

Creative Messages from Beyond

Those who don't believe in magic will never find it.

~Roald Dahl~

Stay Open To The Magic

In this chapter, I share some of the unusual experiences I have had or heard about from my bereavement clients. The fern grew in the pot where for years Grace had asked her husband to plant something. I found the two huge Conch shells while immersed in thoughts and concerns about my patient's two children. The pink cotton balls showed up on my father's birthday. The scooter bell went off every night at the time of her husband's death. Carla's midnight visitor trashed her kitchen just as her husband had for years in their marriage. For years I attempted to explain away the coincidences. I have come to believe that there is life after death and that those who have passed on have the ability to send messages to their loved ones. Now it's time for you to explore what you believe (it's okay if you don't believe what I do). Try to remain open and curious. What you find may surprise you.

Questions to Dance With...

Have you ever had an "unexplainable" experience at the time of someone's death or after someone died?

Describe any coincidences or synchronistic events that you have experienced around the death of a loved one (or any other time, for that matter).

How did it feel when you received these messages or signs? Did you second guess what you were experiencing?

My Expansion

Fully Embracing the Gift of Life

Life shrinks or expands in proportion to one's courage.

~Anaïs Nin~

Facing Death Is Liberating

In this chapter I share my personal evolution and how much my beliefs and life changed as I have embraced the lessons learned from my hospice experiences and began applying them to my life. I have experienced more freedom, authenticity, and joy as I gained clarity in what it was that I wanted in life. My spiritual beliefs have also expanded and grown over the years. May the next series of questions help you to explore where you are in life by taking a gentle inventory of how you are doing and whether there are areas that may need your attention.

Questions to Dance With...

Do you ever feel like life is passing you by or you are running out of time to do what you want to do? Write about what it is you hope to accomplish before the end of your life.

Pick an area in your life that is not ideal and write about it.

Now write in as much detail as possible what you would like it to look like instead.

What steps could you take today to improve this area of your life? List at least five steps and identify when you plan to achieve these steps.

Final Thoughts

Ignoring Death

The fear of death follows from the fear of life.
A man who lives fully is prepared to die at any time.

~Mark Twain~

Do it NOW!

In this final chapter, I share the increasing disconnection people are experiencing in the "age of technology," and the importance of finding ways to nurture these connections. I discussed how important it was to honor those who were dying and for them to acknowledge the people they are leaving behind. I give suggestions on how to "be" with the dying, which is ultimately a way of "being" in the world. It is important to honor people wherever they are on the path, even if their feet are firmly planted in denial.

Throughout *The Final Dance* I talk about my experiences counseling patients at the end of life and listening to their regrets about the things that had not done, the risks they had not taken, and the relationships they had not healed. I share one of the most important lessons I have learned from my patients: Don't put off your dreams, but Do it NOW! I invite you to explore these topics more deeply with the next set of questions.

Questions to Dance With...

How do you feel when you receive acknowledgment?

How do you feel when you give acknowledgment?

Who is someone you would want to acknowledge and what would you want to say to them?

What feelings come up when you think about acknowledging them?

If you were given a prognosis of six months or less to live, what would you want to accomplish? Are there any relationships you would want to heal? Expand upon this.

Healing Exercises

Visualizations and Journaling

To Support You Through Loss or Change

There are several different ways to work with these guided visualizations. These visualizations can be used to take the teachings to a deeper level, and can promote healing if you are going through a transition.

You can read through the text of the visualization first and then go through the process on your own from memory.

You may want to record yourself reading the visualization text aloud. If you choose to read the visualizations yourself pause for 10 seconds when you see the (...) unless otherwise indicated.

You may want to ask someone dear to you to read and record the visualization for you.

You may go to **www.cheryldeines.com** and download my recordings of these guided visualizations.

Whatever route you choose to take, please do the visualizations only when you are in a safe, quiet place. Be sure to give yourself enough time. This is healing work that you are embarking on. Please give yourself the gifts of space and time so that ease and grace can drop in and be your partners on these journeys.

After listening to the visualizations, you can use the following questions to take the experience even deeper.

Your Legacy

This visualization is a great barometer to see where you are in life. After listening to this visualization do the journaling exercise and respond to the questions on the next few pages.

Take a few moments now to write about this experience. Make note of what you were most proud of, the things you regretted, and relationships that might need your attention.

As you experienced your funeral through the visualization, what was being said about you? What accomplishments did they speak of?

If your life were to end today, what regrets would you have? For example, goals you haven't achieved, relationships you haven't healed or trips you haven't taken.

Did looking at the regrets you might have if your life ended today put anything into perspective for you about what you want to accomplish before the end of your life? Elaborate.

What is one thing you long to do that you have been putting off for a more convenient time?

How will you feel if you never get to it?

Are there any relationships you hope to heal in this lifetime? (Share details about this relationship).

Why haven't you taken steps to mend this relationship?

What steps can you take now to start healing this relationship?

Write your obituary. List accomplishments, who is left behind, awards you have received. What would it say in the paper if you died today?

Unfinished Business

Often when a relationship ends, whether it is due to death or a break-up, there are unresolved issues. May this visualization support you in resolving some of what is incomplete between you and someone you have lost. After listening to this guided visualization, answer the following questions:

What did you need to say to your loved one?

What did you need to hear from your loved one? How did it feel to hear this message?

How did your loved one impact your life?

What did you learn from them?

What values or qualities do you possess from having this loved one in your life?

How has your life has been influenced because they were in it?

Are there ways that you intend to or have honored this loved one's life? Write about this.

What were your loved one's parting words?

Reminiscing

Often, when a relationship ends due to death, we romanticize that relationship, remembering only the good. Or, if a relationship ends due to breakup, we can do the opposite, demonizing this relationship. In order to heal from this loss, it's important to remember it all. After listening to this Guided Visualization, answer the following questions:

Who was the person you met on the path?

What brought them joy? What made them laugh out loud?

What made them sad?

What made them angry? What annoyed them?

Write about your biggest disagreement.

Write about your favorite memory of this person.

What made them special to you?

What aspects of this person have you incorporated into your life?

What did you love most about them?

What do you miss most?

Describe your loved one. What color was their eyes, their hair. What was their best physical attribute? What was their favorite color? What was their favorite food?

What was their personality like?

What else comes to mind when you think about this person?

Gentle Awakenings

List songs that would be soothing to wake up to:

After using your music to wake up, write about how it felt to wake up to these songs.

www.ingramcontent.com/pod-product-compliance
Lightning Source LLC
LaVergne TN
LVHW021447080426
835509LV00018B/2192

* 9 7 8 1 7 3 2 1 4 0 0 1 1 *